<u>Dla mamy!</u>

This means "For mom" in Polish. The photo shows my mom and me celebrating my 2nd birthday!

# BROOKLYN ABC
A SCRAPBOOK OF EVERYONE'S FAVORITE BOROUGH

Published by POW! a division of powerHouse Packaging & Supply, Inc.
37 Main Street, Brooklyn, NY 11201-1021
info@POWkidsbooks.com
www.POWkidsbooks.com
www.powerHouseBooks.com
www.powerHousepackaging.com

Library of Congress Control Number: 2014948084
ISBN: 978-1576877517

Book design: Krzysztof Poluchowicz

10 9 8 7 6 5 4 3 2 1

Printed in China

# BROOKLYN ABC

A Scrapbook of Everyone's Favorite Borough

**KRZYSZTOF POLUCHOWICZ**

&

_____

_____

Since you will be adding your own words and pictures to this book, you're my co-author. Put your name right here and let's get started!

Brooklyn is my favorite borough and I hope that you feel the same way after you read this book!

POW!

BROOKLYN, NY

The Wildlife Conservation Society also operates The Bronx Zoo, The Central Park Zoo, The Prospect Park Zoo, and The Queens Zoo. The WCS saves wildlife and wild places around the world.

# A

## IS FOR

# AQUARIUM

The oldest operating aquarium in the United States, and the only one in New York City is in Brooklyn. It opened in 1896 in Battery Park (located at the southern tip of Manhattan), but some 60 years later it was moved to the boardwalk in Coney Island, Brooklyn.

The New York Aquarium is home to more than 350 species of animals who live in or near water. One of them is the black-footed penguin, which sometimes makes its nest out of its own hardened poop!

BRO OKLYN ABC

Did you see any of these animals at the Aquarium? If some of names seem funny, it may be because I made them up! Put a check mark in the column where you think each one belongs. Can you do a drawing of one of the made-up creatures?

| | REAL | NOPE! |
|---|---|---|
| Red-bellied Piranha | | |
| False Clown Anemone Fish | | |
| Candied Crayfish | | |
| Pacific Walrus | | |
| Sea Otter | | |
| Sun-basking Silly Medusa | | |
| California Sea Lion | | |
| Tail-diving Ocean Monkey | | |
| Black-footed Penguin | V | |
| Purple-striped Penguin | | |

Answer on page 56.

A B C D E F G H I J K L M N O P Q R S T U V W X Y Z

Sunset over the Williamsburg Bridge.

Looking at the Manhattan and Brooklyn Bridges from the Williamsburg Bridge.

ANSWERS:
Brooklyn Bridge is a cable-stayed bridge
Pulaski Bridge is a drawbridge
Manhattan Bridge is a suspension bridge
Grand Street Bridge is a swing bridge
Kosciuszko Bridge is a truss bridge

# B IS FOR BRIDGES

How many bridges do you think there are in New York City? Ten? Twenty? A hundred? The correct answer is 2,027 bridges and tunnels! Many of them are in Brooklyn, or connect Brooklyn to other boroughs. The most famous of these is the Brooklyn Bridge, which was opened in 1882 and is the oldest New York City bridge open to both traffic and pedestrians. **The only bridge that is older than the Brooklyn Bridge is the High Bridge, also called the Acqueduct Bridge. It was built in 1846 and it carries . . . water! Isn't that funny?**

For the best views, walk or ride your bike over the Brooklyn Bridge.

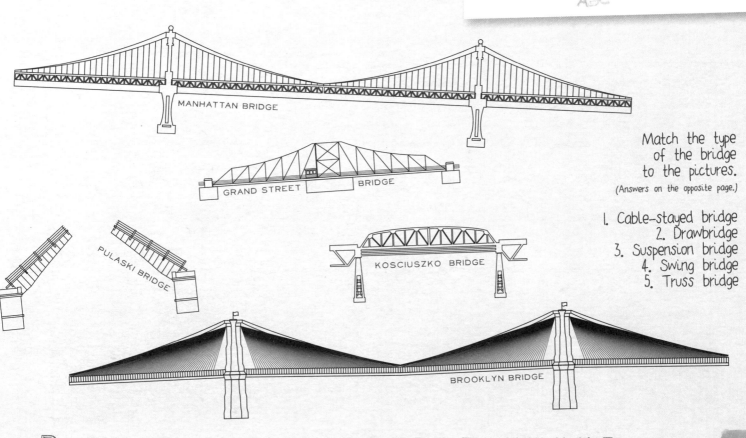

MANHATTAN BRIDGE

GRAND STREET BRIDGE

PULASKI BRIDGE

KOSCIUSZKO BRIDGE

BROOKLYN BRIDGE

Match the type of the bridge to the pictures.
(Answers on the opposite page.)

1. Cable-stayed bridge
2. Drawbridge
3. Suspension bridge
4. Swing bridge
5. Truss bridge

A B C D E F G H I J K L M N O P Q R S T U V W X Y Z

The Cyclone has
a drop of 85 feet
(25.5 m) at its
highest point!

# C

Ahhhhhhhhhhhh
hhhhhhhhhhhhhh
hhhhhhhhhhhh!!!

IS FOR
## CONEY ISLAND
# CYCLONE

LIST ALL THE RIDES THAT YOU
TRIED AT CONEY ISLAND. WHICH ONE
MADE YOU SCREAM THE LOUDEST?

1. _____

2. _____

3. _____

4. _____

5. _____

The Cyclone is one of the most famous roller coasters in the world. It opened in 1927 at Coney Island, on the spot where The Switchback, North America's very first amusement park roller coaster, had once stood. The original cost to ride the Cyclone? Just 25 cents!

It quickly became such a sensation that replicas were built around the world. Today, the Cyclone is a New York City landmark, drawing people from all over to experience the 1-minute, 50-second thrill ride over its famous wooden tracks with their very distinctive clatter. It still delivers an exhilarating ride—the Cyclone has a top speed of 60 miles per hour (100 kph)!

Remember, if you want to ride the Cyclone, you need to be at least 54 inches (137 cm) tall.

A B C D E F G H I J K L M N O P Q R S T U V W X Y Z

The Manhattan Bridge with the Empire State Building framed in the lower arch. (Look at the map on the opposite page to see where this picture was taken.)

# D

## IS FOR
# DUMBO

East River

Brooklyn Bridge Park

Water Street

Front Street

Brooklyn Bridge

Washington Street

York Street

Adams Street

Manhattan Bridge

Pearl Street

Jay Street

On the waterfront in Brooklyn near the bases of two great bridges (the Manhattan and the Brooklyn) sits a neighborhood with a strange name: DUMBO. **It stands for Down Under the Manhattan Bridge Overpass.** The name was coined by the artists who lived there in the 1970s. They loved the area's old factory spaces, cobblestoned streets (actually, the stones are called Belgian blocks), and river views—and they thought if the neighborhood had a silly name, it might prevent developers from coming in and raising prices! Who would want to pay a lot of money to live in a place called DUMBO?

Were they right? What do you think happened?

BRO OKLYN ABC

SOME OTHER NAMES THAT WERE PROPOSED FOR DUMBO ARE:

- DANYA (District Around the Navy Yard Annex)
- Rapailie (after the Dutch family who settled it)
- Olympia (what it was called in the 1700s)
- Gairville (after the cardboard manufacturer who built much of it)
- Walentasville (after the modern developer)

WHAT WOULD YOU RE-NAME YOUR NEIGHBORHOOD?

_____

_____

_____

_____

To read about the bridge in the background, turn to page 47. To find out why people walk on top of the highway, see page 35.

Although the very first automobile had been built only 50 years earlier, by the 1930s, New York City already had serious traffic problems. Manhattan, Queens, and Brooklyn had once been made up of small villages that eventually joined together, and the crazy-quilt patterns of the old streets made it hard to get anywhere fast. **The city decided to build a major roadway to link the boroughs together—they called it the Brooklyn-Queens Connecting Highway.** It began construction in 1939. Under the leadership of engineer Robert Moses, it was finally completed in 1964, by which time it was officially named the Brooklyn-Queens Expressway, or the BQE. It has a two-tiered section under the Brooklyn Heights Promenade (see page 35), crosses the Newtown Creek over the Kosciuszko Bridge (see page 25), and is part of the interstate highway system. On a typical day, nearly 150,000 cars travel on the BQE.

ANSWERS:
Did you guess correctly? The red line is the BQE, and the black line shows the boundaries of Queens and Brooklyn.

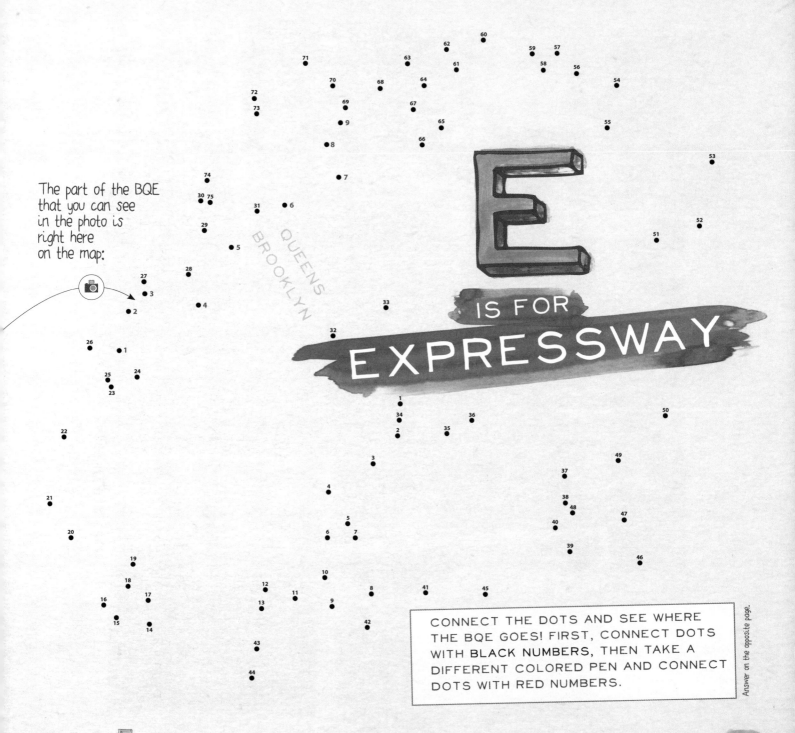

The part of the BQE that you can see in the photo is right here on the map:

QUEENS
BROOKLYN

E IS FOR EXPRESSWAY

CONNECT THE DOTS AND SEE WHERE THE BQE GOES! FIRST, CONNECT DOTS WITH BLACK NUMBERS, THEN TAKE A DIFFERENT COLORED PEN AND CONNECT DOTS WITH RED NUMBERS.

A B C D E F G H I J K L M N O P Q R S T U V W X Y Z

Grand Army Plaza farmers' market on a Saturday in August. What would you buy?

In the summer, you can find the Brooklyn Flea in both Fort Greene and Williamsburg.

# F

When you think about what to buy in Brooklyn, you probably don't think about farm-fresh produce—but in fact, this borough has more than 40 different farmers' markets where farmers from the New York region sell their locally grown products. These markets sell fruit, vegetables, meat, plants, and products made from the local harvests such as cheese, baked goods, maple syrup, and more. The largest farmers' market in Brooklyn occurs at Grand Army Plaza every Saturday all year long, with more than 30 vendors. For a list of all the farmers' markets in Brooklyn, visit www.localharvest.org.

There is another kind of market in Brooklyn that you might like to visit, as well—it's called the Brooklyn Flea—where they sell everything from antiques, collectibles, and vintage clothing to delicious food. Learn more at www.brooklynflea.com.

BRO OKLYN ABC

Answer on page 56.

THESE DELICIOUS VEGGIES ARE HIDDEN BELOW:
ARUGULA, ASPARAGUS, AVOCADO, BROCCOLI, CABBAGE, CARROT, CAULIFLOWER, CUCUMBER, FENNEL, KALE, MUSHROOM, ONION, PEPPER, POTATO, PUMPKIN, RADISH, ZUCCHINI
CAN YOU FIND THEM ALL?

| L | Z | P | C | A | B | B | A | G | E | G | O | O | B | N |
| J | U | E | U | A | L | Y | O | N | L | S | G | B | I | T |
| K | C | B | C | M | U | S | H | R | O | O | M | K | Q | M |
| S | C | J | U | A | J | L | E | Z | H | K | P | E | R | D |
| Y | H | F | M | N | A | M | I | J | Z | M | M | N | A | K |
| V | I | F | B | C | G | V | Q | F | U | W | V | C | D | C |
| E | N | E | E | W | A | A | O | P | L | Y | A | Z | I | O |
| M | I | N | R | M | U | R | S | C | O | O | P | K | S | X |
| C | Q | N | R | H | C | M | U | P | A | T | W | B | H | I |
| A | P | E | P | P | E | R | C | G | A | D | A | E | P | N |
| R | Z | L | E | Z | E | S | F | K | U | R | O | T | R | K |
| R | B | R | O | C | C | O | L | I | D | L | A | M | O | Q |
| O | L | S | G | T | H | R | U | I | J | E | A | G | G | W |
| T | P | H | N | O | N | I | O | N | P | H | Q | K | U | E |
| W | T | E | X | V | K | A | L | E | Q | J | H | O | E | S |

The Gowanus was named
after an Algonquin
Chief, Gowanes, leader
of a local tribe of
Canarsees.
Henry Hudson and
Giovanni da Verrazzano
both sailed on it.
It is 100 feet (30m) wide
and 1.8 miles (3km) long.

16

# IS FOR
# GOWANUS CANAL

If you walk between the Brooklyn neighborhoods of Carroll Gardens and Park Slope, you will cross over a body of water called the Gowanus Canal (also known as Lavender Lake and Perfume Creek.)

Famous for being highly polluted (not to mention stinky), the Gowanus used to be a creek, but when the Industrial Revolution came to Brooklyn, the natural creek was converted into a wood-and-concrete canal. Soon, the canal was a busy industrial corridor. Unfortunately, many businesses dumped pollutants into the water. Those contaminants, along with human waste from the sewage system, left the canal extremely dirty.

Today, the Gowanus Canal is finally scheduled for a major clean-up to be complete by 2023.

BRO OKLYN ABC

**DRAW A CREATURE THAT YOU THINK MIGHT LIVE IN THE GOWANUS. WHAT SPECIAL ABILITIES WOULD IT NEED TO SURVIVE?**

Hanging out at the Gowanus Canal (top left and bottom right), the East River Park in Williamsburg (top right), and the Prospect Park (bottom left.)

# H IS FOR HIPSTERS

Brooklyn is a creative place that draws all kinds of people together—and sometimes, a certain neighborhood will attract certain kinds of people who give it a special flavor. In the Brooklyn neighborhood of Williamsburg, which is famous for its creative community, one species of person that has become a pop-culture phenomenon is known as a "hipster." While it's a generalization, there are some qualities that identify the young people who are known as hipsters. In fashion, hipsters tend to have a liking for vintage or thrift-store fashion and ironic looks like old-fashioned eyeglasses or lots of facial hair. Hipsters value locally sourced and organic food and artisanal or hand-made products; they don't like big brands and mega-stores. They are usually environmentally conscious and progressive politically. Sound good to you? Move to Brooklyn!

PULL TOGETHER A HIPSTER OUTFIT–ADD COLORS AND PATTERNS TO MAKE IT STYLISH.

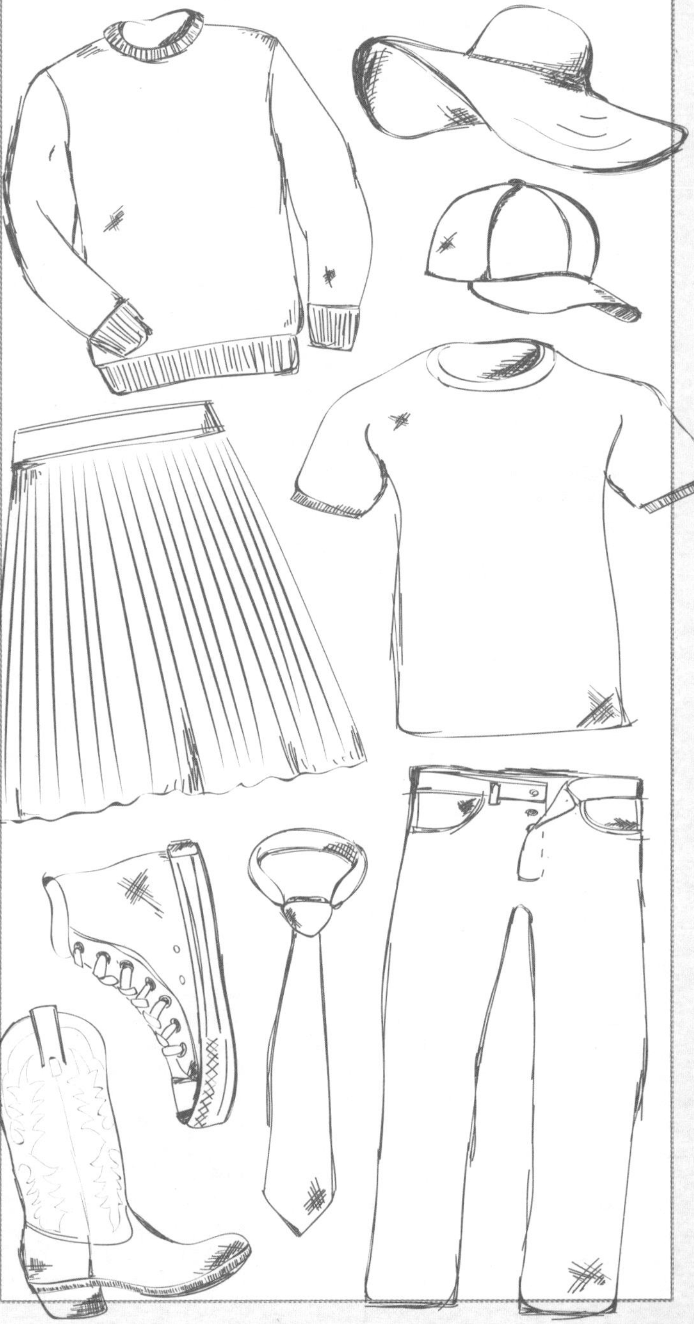

Founded in 1898, Kentile Floors made floor tiles from cork, rubber, and vinyl. The sign went up in 1949 and was taken down in 2014.

The Domino Sugar Factory was built in 1856, then rebuilt after a fire in 1882. Soon it will be converted into living spaces.

Conveyor belts moved the sugar from the refinery to the storage areas.

# I IS FOR INDUSTRY

Back in the 1800s, Brooklyn was a major industrial center, which means it had lots of factories producing manufactured goods of all sorts. The biggest industry in Brooklyn was sugar refining—Brooklyn produced more than half the sugar in the United States! Other things made in Brooklyn included ships, cardboard boxes, pencils, floor tiles, bricks, ice, clocks, beer, baked goods, books, clothing, glue, and cigars. By the 1950s, however, many of these manufacturers had closed down or moved away from the city. Today, many of the factories that once held Brooklyn's industries are gone, while others have been given landmark status, and still others have been transformed into new kinds of structures, from apartment buildings to galleries and stores.

BROOKLYN ABC

One of the more delicious items manufactured in Brooklyn (since the early 1900s) is Fox's U-Bet Chocolate Syrup, a key ingredient in the iconic Brooklyn treat known as the Egg Cream. It's a frothy chocolate-y drink, and you can make it! Here's how:

## THE ORIGINAL BROOKLYN EGG-CREAM

- CHILL A TALL, 8-OUNCE (240 ML) GLASS
- SPOON IN 1 INCH (2.5 CM) U-BET CHOCOLATE SYRUP
- ADD 1/2 CUP (120 ML) WHOLE MILK
- POUR IN SELTZER WATER TO ALMOST THE TOP OF THE GLASS, WHILE STIRRING VIGOROUSLY TO CREATE A FOAMY HEAD

↑ Jane's Carousel has 48 horses and 1,200 twinkling lights.

← If you don't want to ride one of the horses, the carousel also has 2 beautiful chariots.

IS FOR

# JANE'S CAROUSEL

In a transparent pavilion in Brooklyn Bridge Park overlooking the East River, you will find a glorious merry-go-round known as Jane's Carousel. It's named for Jane Walentas, who spent years carefully researching and restoring this antique beauty that dates back to 1922, when the Philadelphia Toboggan Company originally built it for a park in Ohio. Jane worked on it for many years, scraping off the original paint, researching colors, and even arranging for the horses' fittings to be gilded with paint made from 24-carat gold! When it was done, Jane and her husband asked French architect Jean Nouvel to design a home for the carousel, and now you can visit and enjoy a ride in any weather.

Brooklyn also has 2 other historic carousels: in Prospect Park, the Carmel-Murphy Carousel dates back to 1912, and Coney Island boasts the B&B Carousel, which was built in 1919.

HERE IS A MERRY-GO-ROUND-HORSE THAT NEEDS TO BE NAMED AND DECORATED! IMAGINE THAT YOU ARE RESTORING AN ORIGINAL WORK FROM THE PAST, OR CREATE YOUR OWN, MODERN DESIGN!

MY HORSE'S MAME IS:

A B C D E F G H I J K L M N O P Q R S T U V W X Y Z

## IS FOR
# KOŚCIUSZKO

The Kosciuszko Bridge, Kosciuszko Street, Kosciuszko Station on the J line, Kosciuszko Pool—there are a lot of places in Brooklyn named after Kościuszko. Who was he?

Tadeusz Kościuszko was born in Poland in 1746 and came to America in 1776 to help the colonies fight for their independence. A trained engineer, he quickly set to work building fortifications. In 1783, George Washington appointed Kościuszko a Brigadier General in the Continental Army.

Upon reading the Declaration of Independence, Kościuszko was so moved by its values that he decided to meet Thomas Jefferson; they became great friends, and Jefferson said of him, "He is as pure a son of liberty as I have ever known."

Kościuszko believed in freedom for all. In his will he directed that his money be spent on freeing slaves and paying for their education.

BRO OKLYN ABC

KOŚCIUSZKO IS ALSO FAMOUS FOR WRITING *ADVICE TO A YOUTH*, A SET OF RULES FOR LIVING, INCLUDING:

- wake up at 4am in the summer and 6am in the winter
- never, ever lie
- think before speaking out loud
- respect your parents and elders
- always look for an opportunity to be useful
- be polite and considerate to everybody
- be helpful to the unfortunate

DO YOU LIVE BY THESE RULES?
WHAT RULE WOULD YOU ADD?

------------------------------------

------------------------------------

A B C D E F G H I J **K** L M N O P Q R S T U V W X Y Z

Love locks on the
Brooklyn Bridge
with the skyline
of the Lower
Manhattan in the
distance. If you'd
like to know more
about the skyline,
turn to page 41.

# L IS FOR LOVE LOCKS

YOU MAY NOT BE ABLE TO BREAK A LOVE LOCK BUT MAYBE YOU CAN UNLOCK THIS CODED MESSAGE:

| 9 | | 12 | 15 | 22 | 5 |
|---|---|----|----|----|---|
| □ | | □ | □ | □ | □ |

| 2 | 18 | 15 | 15 | 12 | 25 | 14 |
|---|----|----|----|----|----|----|
| □ | □ | □ | □ | □ | □ | □ |

Here's a clue: A=1

YOU CAN DEVELOP YOUR OWN SECRET CODE BY ASSIGNING DIFFERENT NUMBERS TO THE LETTERS (SUGGESTION: A=26) AND SEND SECRET MESSAGES TO YOUR FRIENDS.

Answer on the opposite page.

If you walk across the Brooklyn Bridge, you will see thousands of combination locks and padlocks attached to virtually every part of the bridge. What is going on here? These are the famous love locks! They are affixed to the bridge by lovers who write their names on the locks, toss the keys into the river, and leave the locks there ever after as symbols of "unbreakable" love. This romantic tradition began with bridges in Europe and quickly migrated to Brooklyn. People come from around the world to declare their love and leave a lock behind to express their everlasting devotion. Unfortunately, those locks are pretty heavy, and their combined weight may become a danger to the bridge's stability. But for now, when you see the locks, you'll know you're looking at a whole lotta love!

BRO OKLYN ABC

A B C D E F G H I J K L M N O P Q R S T U V W X Y Z

AN ARTIFACT IS SOMETHING THAT PEOPLE MAKE, AND USE. ART IS ALSO SOMETHING THAT PEOPLE CREATE, BUT THEY USE IT TO EXPRESS IMAGINATION OR EMOTION. DO YOU SEE THE DIFFERENCE? TRY TO THINK OF SOME EXAMPLES OF EACH.

In a 1923 show, the Brooklyn Museum was the first in America to display African objects as art. Before that, they were considered just "artifacts."

# IS FOR MUSEUM

Find the best way from the Museum Entrance to The Mummy Chamber. Try to see as many galleries as possible on your way!

The Brooklyn Museum is New York City's second largest museum (Can you guess which is the largest? It's the Metropolitan Museum of Art in Manhattan.) Set next to the magnificent Brooklyn Botanic Garden, the museum's imposing columns were designed in 1893 by the renowned architects McKim, Mead, and White. In 2004, a new glass and concrete entrance pavilion was added, featuring a public plaza where visitors can sit and a new fountain with "dancing" water jets. Inside the museum there is a wonderful collection of art with more than 1.5 million objects! There are ancient Egyptian masterpieces, African art, European paintings, period rooms, and contemporary art.

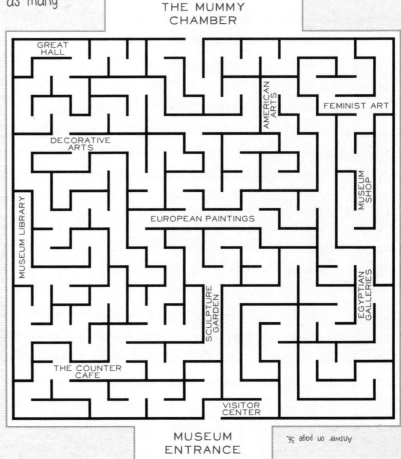

THE MUMMY CHAMBER

GREAT HALL

DECORATIVE ARTS

AMERICAN ARTS

FEMINIST ART

MUSEUM LIBRARY

MUSEUM SHOP

EUROPEAN PAINTINGS

EGYPTIAN GALLERIES

SCULPTURE GARDEN

THE COUNTER CAFE

VISITOR CENTER

MUSEUM ENTRANCE

Answer on page 56.

A B C D E F G H I J K L M N O P Q R S T U V W X Y Z

The Brooklyn Navy Yard
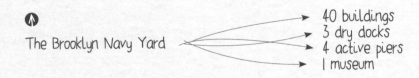
→ 40 buildings
→ 3 dry docks
→ 4 active piers
→ 1 museum

# N

## IS FOR NAVY YARD

DRAW A SHIP THAT COULD HAVE BEEN BUILT AT THE NAVY YARD:

NAME YOUR SHIP: _____

Once a private shipyard set on the shoreline of the East River at Wallabout Bay, the Brooklyn Navy Yard has seen dramatic changes over its more than 200-year history. From the early 1800s until 1966, it was one of the nation's busiest naval manufacturers—among many ships built there was the ill-fated warship *USS Maine*, which sunk off the coast of Cuba in 1898. During World War II, the navy yard employed more than 70,000 men and women to build and repair cruisers, destroyers, and battleships. After WWII, the shipyard went into decline, and in 1966, it was decommissioned.

Today, the Navy Yard is once again humming with industry! Some 300 diverse businesses (with a focus on sustainable enterprise), have set up shop there, including the largest rooftop farm in the country, a huge movie and television studio, distilleries, furniture makers, and more. Visitors can tour the site (be sure to check out the crumbling mansions of Admiral's Row) and learn more about Brooklyn's industrial history at BLDG 92, the navy yard's own museum.

BRO OKLYN ABC

This photo was taken at the beach at Coney Island. Do you remember what famous landmark is there? If you don't, go back to page 9.

# IS FOR
# OCEAN

ON THE MAP,
CAN YOU LOCATE
ALL THE BROOKLYN
BEACHES? WHICH
ONE IS YOUR
FAVORITE?

Answer on page 56.

When you think of Brooklyn, you probably don't think of ocean breezes and sandy beaches. It's easy to forget that Brooklyn is actually on an island—Long Island— and Brooklyn's southwest border is right on the Atlantic Ocean! When Hurricane Sandy hit in October, 2012, Brooklynites got a serious reminder that the ocean is nearby. In calmer weather, Brooklyn's ocean beaches at Coney Island, Manhattan Beach, and Brighton Beach are open to the public and offer sand, surf, and swimming plus a chance to watch the tides roll in and out, and to learn about the great variety of marine life in Brooklyn's waters. You might even see a mermaid!

ARE THERE SHARKS IN BROOKLYN?
Yes! Many species of coastal sharks have been spotted in the waters off Coney Island, including makos, threshers, blue sharks—and the occasional great white!

CAN YOU SEE WHALES IN BROOKLYN?
Yes again! Humpback, fin, and right whales visit Brooklyn on their way from their southern breeding grounds to their feeding grounds off New England.

A B C D E F G H I J K L M N O P Q R S T U V W X Y Z

Do you remember what's under the Promenade? If you don't, go back to page 13.

ANSWERS:
Cranberry, Pineapple, Orange, and Poplar.

# P IS FOR PROMENADE

Take a walk along the Brooklyn Heights Promenade and you will discover one of the best places in Brooklyn to see the lower Manhattan skyline. Here, in one of Brooklyn's oldest neighborhoods, the elevation is so high that a walk down the Promenade ensures spectacular views of Governors Island, the Statue of Liberty, the Upper New York Bay, the financial district, the Brooklyn Bridge, and the East River.

The Promenade was erected in 1950 to protect the neighborhood from the noise of the newly built Brooklyn-Queens Expressway.

Where the Promenade is today, once there were gardens and the backyards of the brownstone houses that still stand there. Today, visitors to the Promenade can enjoy the marvelous views day and evening.

"There may be finer views than this in the world, but I don't believe it."
—ABE LINCOLN, 1864

BRO OKLYN ABC

BROOKLYN HEIGHTS HAS SOME OF THE MOST INTERESTING STREET NAMES. SEE IF YOU CAN SOLVE THIS PUZZLE TO FIND OUT WHAT THEY ARE.

RBNERAYRC _ _ _ _ _ _ _ _ _

IPNAPLEEP _ _ _ _ _ _ _ _

GENRAO _ _ _ _ _ _

ARPOPL _ _ _ _ _

Answer on the opposite page.

What the president saw in the mid–19th century was of course quite a different view from what we see today. There were no skyscrapers in Manhattan and the Brooklyn Bridge was only in the planning stages.

A B C D E F G H I J K L M N O **P** Q R S T U V W X Y Z

ANSWERS:
1. DeKalb Av
2. Atlantic Av–
   Barclays Ct
3. 7 Av
4. Prospect Park
5. Church Av
6. Parkside Av
7. Beverley Rd
8. Cortelyou Rd
9. Newkirk Plaza
10. Avenue H

1. Avenue J
12. Avenue M
13. Kings Hwy
14. Avenue U
15. Neck Rd
16. Sheepshead Bay
17. Brighton Beach
18. Ocean Pkwy
19. West 8 St–
    NY Aquarium
20. Coney Island–
    Stillwell Av

# Q

## IS FOR
# Q TRAIN

Manhattan

Queens

ASTORIA
DITMARS BLVD
ASTORIA
BLVD
5 AV/
59 ST   LEXINGTON
AV/59 ST
30 AV
57 ST–7 AV
BROADWAY
49 ST
36 AV
TIMES SQ–
42 ST
39 AV
34 ST
HERALD SQ
QUEENSBORO
PLAZA

UNION SQ

CANAL ST

The Q train, better known in Brooklyn as the Brighton Beach Express (and in Manhattan as the Broadway Express) runs from Ditmars Boulevard in the Astoria section of Queens through Manhattan all the way to Coney Island, Brooklyn. The Q line, with its variety of stations above and below-ground, is a great way to explore the New York City subway system. The earliest parts of the Q line date back to 1878, when the steam railroad trains of the Brooklyn, Flatbush, and Coney Island Railway started running from Prospect Park to the Brighton Beach Hotel on Coney Island. A series of extensions took the line to Manhattan by the early 1900s, and the New York City Subway opened in 1904 with 28 stations. The BMT (Brooklyn-Manhattan Transit) subway service, including the Brighton Beach line, officially began August 1, 1920. In 1960, the line was designated Q.

### DO YOU KNOW THE Q?

Fill in the names of all Q train stations in Brooklyn. Can you do it without looking at the answers on the opposite page?

1. _____
2. _____
3. _____
4. _____
5. _____
6. _____
7. _____
8. _____
9. _____
10. _____
11. _____
12. _____
13. _____
14. _____
15. _____
16. _____
17. _____
18. _____
19. _____
20. _____

BRO
OKLYN
ABC

A B C D E F G H I J K L M N O P Q R S T U V W X Y Z

Places to get a snack in Red Hook:

◀ Steve's Key Lime Pies

▶ Baked

# R IS FOR RED HOOK

CAN YOU FIND THESE 16 WORDS THAT RELATE TO THE BATTLE OF BROOKLYN?
ARMY, AUGUST, BATTERY, BAYONET, BRITISH, BROOKLYN, DEFIANCE, GEORGE, HOWE, INDEPENDENCE, MUSKET, REDCOATS, REDHOOK, RETREAT, SOLDIER, WASHINGTON

| I | P | Z | U | M | X | S | F | K | U | A | Z | J | K | Y |
|---|---|---|---|---|---|---|---|---|---|---|---|---|---|---|
| N | G | Z | M | U | S | K | E | T | Z | T | Q | N | S | X |
| G | I | B | L | R | S | D | A | V | S | L | T | Y | S | O |
| W | N | G | R | X | A | E | D | U | Z | W | M | T | E | N |
| H | D | P | C | I | R | S | G | U | A | R | A | W | J | Q |
| P | E | Y | S | T | T | U | T | Y | A | O | B | A | O | B |
| B | P | R | E | O | A | I | R | V | C | D | P | S | B | S |
| A | E | R | E | P | L | E | S | D | G | E | R | H | Z | E |
| Y | N | S | F | D | T | D | E | H | O | F | R | I | V | V |
| O | D | U | G | T | H | R | I | X | T | I | M | N | P | G |
| N | E | S | A | C | B | O | H | E | W | A | J | G | J | V |
| E | N | B | P | K | N | T | O | E | R | N | V | T | B | U |
| T | C | P | K | J | K | J | A | K | T | C | H | O | W | E |
| Z | E | I | R | G | E | O | R | G | E | E | Q | N | B | S |
| K | B | R | O | O | K | L | Y | N | J | B | S | O | Z | L |

Answer on page 56.

In 1636, Dutch colonists settled a swampy portion of the south Brooklyn shoreline and called it Roode Hoek ("red point") after the red clay soil of the peninsula that pointed out into the harbor. During the American Revolution, the Continental forces constructed a defensive battlement at Red Hook Point known as Fort Defiance, which played a crucial role in helping George Washington's troops during the Battle of Brooklyn. From the mid-1800s until the 1960s, Red Hook was a thriving freight port. Today, the old warehouses of industrial-era Brooklyn have been transformed into thriving retail, residential, and artisanal spaces, and Red Hook is a destination for tourists, especially those who want to learn about Red Hook's history at the Waterfront Museum or to see a great view (full front) of New York Harbor's Statue of Liberty!

Here is the view from Williamsburg's East River Park.

Sunset over the Financial District from the Manhattan Bridge.

And here is the view from the bridge to the Promenade.

ANSWERS:
1. The Empire State Building
2. One World Trade Center
3. Bank of America Tower
4. Chrysler Building
5. The Statue of Liberty
6. The Woolworth Building

# S IS FOR SKYLINE

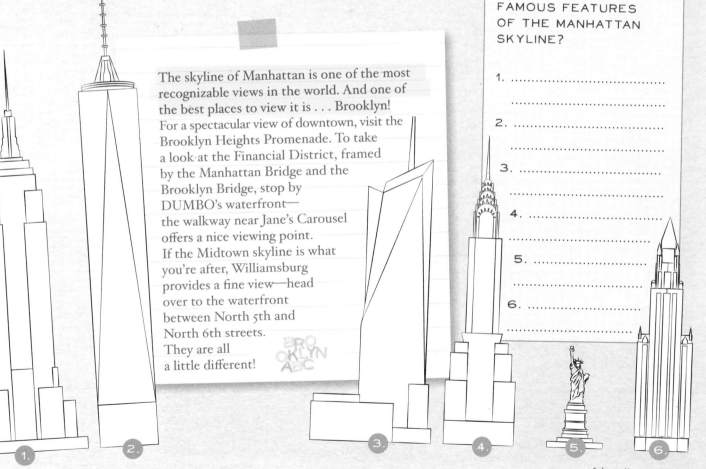

The skyline of Manhattan is one of the most recognizable views in the world. And one of the best places to view it is . . . Brooklyn! For a spectacular view of downtown, visit the Brooklyn Heights Promenade. To take a look at the Financial District, framed by the Manhattan Bridge and the Brooklyn Bridge, stop by DUMBO's waterfront— the walkway near Jane's Carousel offers a nice viewing point. If the Midtown skyline is what you're after, Williamsburg provides a fine view—head over to the waterfront between North 5th and North 6th streets. They are all a little different!

BRO OKLYN ABC

CAN YOU NAME THESE FAMOUS FEATURES OF THE MANHATTAN SKYLINE?

1. ......................................
......................................
2. ......................................
......................................
3. ......................................
......................................
4. ......................................
......................................
5. ......................................
......................................
6. ......................................
......................................

1.    2.    3.    4.    5.    6.

Answer on the opposite page.

↑ ↓ Crowds flock to the Brooklyn Botanic Garden during springtime.

← Thousands celebrate the Brooklyn Bridge's birthday, on May 24th.

# T

## IS FOR TOURISTS

Can you guess how many of the more than 55 million tourists who visit New York City every year cross over a bridge or travel through a tunnel to see Brooklyn? More than 15 million! Many of them walk (or bike) across the Brooklyn Bridge, Manhattan Bridge, or Williamsburg Bridge. Others hop on the subway. And what do they do when they get here? You've already seen some of the top attractions in this book—but there are lots more, large and small, that I couldn't write about but that are worth a visit, including the Soldiers' and Sailor's Memorial Arch at Grand Army Plaza; the beautiful Prospect Park, famously designed by Calvert Vaux and Frederick Law Olmsted; the newer, modern Brooklyn Bridge Park; the winding lanes of Green-Wood Cemetery; Brooklyn Botanic Garden, with its marvelous cherry trees and Japanese gardens; the New York Transit Museum, where you can see old subway cars; Weeksville Heritage Center, once a thriving African-American community; and the Wyckoff Farmhouse Museum, which is New York City's oldest house!

BRO OKLYN ABC

LIST YOUR TOP 5 PLACES TO VISIT IN BROOKLYN:

1. .....................................

2. .....................................

3. .....................................

4. .....................................

5. .....................................

↑ Plymouth Church in Brooklyn Heights with a statue of Henry Ward Beecher.

ERECTED TO THE GLORY OF GOD AND
THE ADORNMENT OF MY BELOVED CITY

ANSWERS:
1.E, 2.F, 3.A, 4.G,
5.D, 6.H, 7.C, 8.B

# U IS FOR UNDERGROUND RAILROAD

Did you know that a simple Brooklyn church, established in 1847, was once a major hub of the Underground Railroad, the secret network of anti-slavery activists who helped thousands of slaves flee the American South before the Civil War? It's true—Plymouth Church, in Brooklyn Heights, presided over by the fiery abolitionist Henry Ward Beecher, was the "Grand Central Depot" of the New York branch of the Underground Railroad, hiding escaped slaves and helping move them north to safety and freedom. Beecher (who was admired by none other than Abraham Lincoln) fought against slavery publicly from his pulpit, while privately aiding fugitives by hiding them in the spaces under the main church rooms. Though there were other Brooklyn "conductors," due to the secrecy required, there was little documentation of their activities—leaving Plymouth Church as the only documented remaining depot on the Underground Railroad.

BROOKLYN ABC

AGENTS WHO WORKED ON BEHALF OF THE UNDERGROUND RAILROAD HAD TO USE THE UTMOST SECRECY TO AVOID GETTING CAUGHT, AND SO THEY COMMUNICATED USING CODE WORDS. CAN YOU CONNECT THE CODE WORD TO ITS MEANING?

1. Baggage
2. Conductor
3. Depot or Station
4. Drinking Gourd
5. Freight
6. Moses
7. Promised Land
8. Stockholder

A. A safe house
B. A supporter who donated to the cause
C. Canada
D. Fugitive slaves
E. Fugitive slaves transported by agents
F. Someone who escorted the fugitives
G. The Big Dipper
H. The famous conductor Harriet Tubman

Answer on the opposite page.

A B C D E F G H I J K L M N O P Q R S T U V W X Y Z

When it opened in 1964, the double-decker Verrazano-Narrows Bridge was the longest suspension bridge in the world; today its span is still the longest of any bridge in the Americas. The Verrazano spans the Narrows, which form the entrance to New York Harbor, and connects two boroughs, with one end in Brooklyn at Fort Hamilton, and the other in Staten Island at Fort Wadsworth. It was named after the first European to enter New York Harbor, the Florentine explorer Giovanni da Verrazzano. With its enormous towers reaching 693 feet (210 m) high, the bridge is visible from many points in Brooklyn. Interestingly, it is affected by the climate—in the summertime, the Verrazano is actually 12 feet (3.6 m) lower than it is in the winter! The bridge is also the starting point of the New York Marathon, but that is the only time that pedestrians are allowed to cross it.

# V IS FOR VERRAZANO–NARROWS BRIDGE

VOYAGES OF DISCOVERY!

ICELAND

Henry Hudson

ENGLAND

Jacques Cartier

FRANCE

Samuel de Champlain

Giovanni da Verrazano

PORTUGAL

SPAIN

NORTH AMERICA

ATLANTIC OCEAN

Christopher Columbus

AFRICA

GULF OF MEXICO

HERE ARE THE ROUTES TAKEN BY SOME OF THE FIRST EUROPEAN EXPLORERS WHO CAME TO THE NEW WORLD. MARK THE ROUTE YOU WOULD TAKE!

A B C D E F G H I J K L M N O P Q R S T U V W X Y Z

Look up at the rooftops in Brooklyn, and what do you see? Water towers, those wooden cones that sit atop nearly every building higher than six stories tall. What's up with those? These water towers hold drinking water for the buildings below them (and provide water for fighting fires, as well.) They came into use starting in the late 1800s, when tall buildings were becoming the norm, and pumps couldn't push water high enough to reach the upper floors. Originally built like wooden barrels, the water towers were held together with cables and often leaked when first filled. Eventually, the water thoroughly soaked the wood, which swelled, making the barrels water-tight. Estimates put the number of water towers in all of New York City at between 12,000 and 17,000. Often decorated by artists and frequently snapped by photographers, they have become iconic symbols of Brooklyn's residential skyline.

BRO
OKLYN
ABC

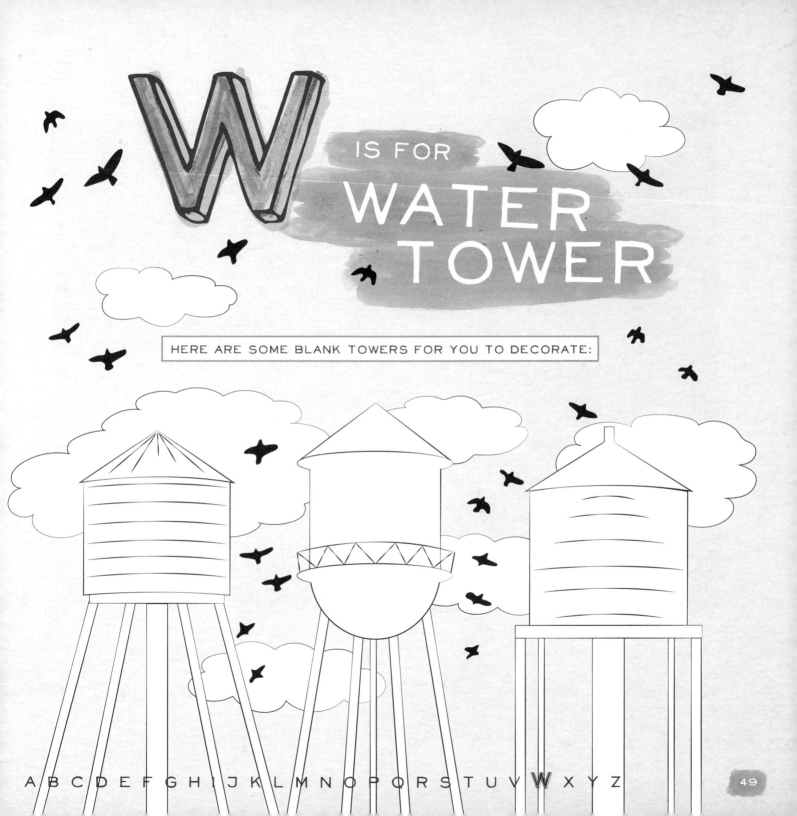

# W

IS FOR

# WATER
# TOWER

HERE ARE SOME BLANK TOWERS FOR YOU TO DECORATE:

A B C D E F G H I J K L M N O P Q R S T U V W X Y Z

A school crossing sign on DeKalb Avenue in Bushwick with the DeKalb Library branch of the Brooklyn Public Library in the background.

New York City's public school system is the largest in the nation, with more than 1.1 million students attending school here! In the borough of Brooklyn alone, there are more than 300,000 students studying at more than 1,000 different elementary, middle, and high schools. Among all those students, more than 171 different languages are spoken! The city employs more than 21,000 teachers to educate the students, more than 400 principals to run the schools, and as many as 2,000 crossing guards to get all those kids across the busy streets safely, every day!

IS FOR
X-ING

HOW TO SAY "school" IN SOME OF THE MANY LANGUAGES SPOKEN IN BROOKLYN:

| | | |
|---|---|---|
| 1. SZKOŁA | | ARABIC |
| 2. XUÉXIÀO | | BENGALI |
| 3. KOULUN | | FILIPINO |
| 4. LÉKOL | | FINNISH |
| 5. OKUL | | FRENCH |
| 6. ESCUELA | | GERMAN |
| 7. MADRASA | | HAITIAN CREOLE |
| 8. ÉCOLE | | HAUSA |
| 9. SCOLASTICO | | ITALIAN |
| 10. ILE-IWE | | MANDARIN CHINESE |
| 11. MAKARANTA | | POLISH |
| 12. SKULA | | RUSSIAN |
| 13. SHKOLA | | SPANISH |
| 14. SCHULE | | TURKISH |
| 15. PAARALAN | | YIDDISH |
| 16. SHUL | | YORUBA |

Answer on the opposite page.

A B C D E F G H I J K L M N O P Q R S T U V W X Y Z

# Y IS FOR YARMULKE

*Yarmulke* is a Yiddish word for the circular cap worn by members of the Jewish faith. New York City has the largest Jewish population in the world outside Israel, with some half a million Jewish people living in Brooklyn. Jewish culture has influenced the city in many ways, particularly in cuisine (bagels, lox, and chicken soup are just a few of the Jewish specialties that New Yorkers of all varieties love to eat.) Several Brooklyn neighborhoods are home to thriving Jewish communities, including Borough Park, Crown Heights, and Williamsburg, where you are likely to see the distinctively dressed members of the Hasidic sects, who are very strict in their observances.

BRO OKLYN ABC

JEWISH CULTURE HAS GIVEN US MANY DELICIOUS FOODS THAT YOU CAN FIND IN BROOKLYN. PUT A CHECK MARK NEXT TO ALL THE ONES YOU'VE TRIED.

- [ ] BABKA: A pastry with chocolate or cinnamon-sugar filling; it means "grandmother" in Polish.

- [ ] BAGEL: A hard, chewy roll with a hole in the middle; from a Yiddish word for ring.

- [ ] BIALY: A soft roll with onion and poppy seeds in the center; from the town of Bialystock.

- [ ] BORSCHT: A soup made from beets; from a Russian word for soup.

- [ ] HAMANTASHEN: triangle-shaped cookies filled with jam; named after a villain in the Bible.

- [ ] KNISH: a savory turnover filled with potato, meat, or veggies; from a Yiddish word for pastry.

- [ ] LOX: smoked or cured salmon; from the Yiddish word for salmon.

The pool where
Stella and
Beebe live.

## Z

IS FOR

# ZOO

Kangaroos in Prospect Park? It's true! One of the many delights of Prospect Park is the Prospect Park Zoo, where peacocks roam freely, sea lions cavort year-round in their circular pool, a clan of hamadryas baboons entertains crowds, and visitors can walk the Discovery Trail with prairie dogs, red pandas, dingos, an emu, and yes, even kangaroos. The tradition of a zoo in the park dates back to the 1890s, when the Menagerie held a rather odd assortment of donated animals, including bears, a sacred cow, and a flock of sheep that were used to maintain the grass in the park's meadows. The current zoo opened in 1993 under the auspices of the Wildlife Conservation Society (which also operates the Aquarium, see page 5).

ALL THE ANIMALS AT THE ZOO HAVE NAMES, AND SOME OF THEM WERE CHOSEN BY VISITORS LIKE YOU!

Sea lions – Stella and Beebe
Baboons – Simon, Moja, and Bole
Pallas Cats – Boris and Natasha
Otters – Dixie, Oogie, and Erin
Sheep – Fred and Ginger

WHAT WOULD YOU NAME THESE GOATS?

...................................................................

A B C D E F G H I J K L M N O P Q R S T U V W X Y Z

**PAGE 5:**

THE MADE-UP
ANIMALS ARE:

Candied Crayfish
Sun-basking Silly Medusa
Tail-diving Ocean Monkey
Purple-striped Penguin

WHICH ONE DID
YOU DRAW?

**PAGE 15:**

| L | Z | P | C | A | B | B | A | G | E | G | O | O | B | N |
|---|---|---|---|---|---|---|---|---|---|---|---|---|---|---|
| J | U | E | U | A | L | Y | O | N | L | S | G | B | I | T |
| K | C | B | C | M | U | S | H | R | O | O | M | K | Q | M |
| S | C | J | U | A | J | L | E | Z | H | K | P | E | R | D |
| Y | H | F | M | N | A | M | I | J | Z | M | M | N | A | K |
| V | I | F | B | C | G | V | Q | F | U | W | V | C | D | C |
| E | N | E | E | W | A | A | O | P | L | Y | A | Z | I | O |
| M | I | N | R | M | U | R | S | C | O | O | P | K | S | X |
| C | Q | N | R | H | C | M | U | P | A | T | W | B | H | I |
| A | P | E | P | P | E | R | C | G | A | D | A | E | P | N |
| R | Z | L | E | Z | E | S | F | K | U | R | O | T | R | K |
| R | B | R | O | C | C | O | L | I | D | L | A | M | O | Q |
| O | L | S | G | T | H | R | U | I | J | E | A | G | G | W |
| T | P | H | N | O | N | I | O | N | P | H | Q | K | U | E |
| W | T | E | X | V | K | A | L | E | Q | J | H | O | E | S |

**PAGE 29:**

**PAGE 33:**

Coney
Island
Beach

Brighton
Beach

Manhattan
Beach

**PAGE 39:**

| I | P | Z | U | M | X | S | F | K | U | A | Z | J | K | Y |
|---|---|---|---|---|---|---|---|---|---|---|---|---|---|---|
| N | G | Z | M | U | S | K | E | T | Z | T | Q | N | S | X |
| G | I | B | L | R | S | D | A | V | S | L | T | Y | S | O |
| W | N | G | R | X | A | E | D | U | Z | W | M | T | E | N |
| H | D | P | C | I | R | S | G | U | A | R | A | W | J | Q |
| P | E | Y | S | T | T | U | T | Y | A | O | B | A | O | B |
| B | P | R | E | O | A | I | R | V | C | D | P | S | B | S |
| A | E | R | E | P | L | E | S | D | G | E | R | H | Z | E |
| Y | N | S | F | D | T | D | E | H | O | F | R | I | V | V |
| O | D | U | G | T | H | R | I | X | T | I | M | N | P | G |
| N | E | S | A | C | B | O | H | E | W | A | J | G | J | V |
| E | N | B | P | K | N | T | O | E | R | N | V | T | B | U |
| T | C | P | K | J | K | J | A | K | T | C | H | O | W | E |
| Z | E | I | R | G | E | O | R | G | E | E | Q | N | B | S |
| K | B | R | O | O | K | L | Y | N | J | B | S | O | Z | L |

I would like to thank:

My publisher and editor Sharyn Rosart, whose excitement, kindness, and parenting wisdom made this book possible,

Andrzej Kińczyk, who patiently agreed and waited all the countless times, when I said, "Hey, can we stop here, I'd like to take a photo,"

Jacob Pastrovich, who has been an eager companion, supporter, and . . . model,

and Yuka Anziano, who is making everything possible.

And, of course, thanks to everyone at powerHouse Books and POW!

BRO
OKLYN
ABC